Renew

Principles of Change
for a Better Life

By Bryan Hudson, Th.B., B.S., M.S.

PUBLISHED BY
visionBooks & Media

www.VisionBooksMedia.com
www.BryanHudson.com

Contents

Introduction

Welcome! This is a devotional book about personal change and positive development. We want to change for the better and change in ways that honor God and empower us to get the most out of life. Here is a foundational Scripture that we will consider on several occasions.

And do not be conformed to this world, but be transformed by the renewing of your mind, that you may prove what is that good and acceptable and perfect will of God. (Romans 12:2)

To be "transformed" is to be changed in a progressive manner. It would not be wrong to think that becoming a Christian is the moment that produced all the change. However, becoming a Christian was the *beginning* of change and growth. Someone can build an airplane and put a pilot's uniform on a person, but until that person is trained, learns how to control the airplane, and takes the controls, he cannot be certified as a pilot. A Christian is more than a title, surroundings, and a "uniform." Jesus called us disciples, which means "students" or "learners." This is the attitude we should adopt. Learning produces the best kind of change.

According to what Paul wrote, we are "transformed" or changed by what happens in the mind. Specifically, we want to experience a change in thinking and understanding that helps align ourselves with God and with the best experiences of life. This devotional book will focus on the mind and consider the benefits of renewal and higher thinking.

To believers who struggle in their faith-walk, I suggest that you continue reading. Discovery is a good thing!

To those who consider themselves strong in faith, I suggest that you continue reading. Discovery is *still* a good thing! Remember that "faith comes by hearing" (active), not by having heard (passive).

How to use this devotional:

Following each reading, complete the following:

1. Respond to Reflection Question.

2. Write down any insights you gain from the Scripture reading and commentary.

3. Write down any action items based on what you have read.

4. Continue your prayer and devotional time as the Lord directs you.

Day 1
What is the Mind?

According to Webster's dictionary, the mind is: *"That element of a person that enables them to be aware of the world and their experiences, to think, and to feel; the faculty of consciousness and thought."*

This is a good definition, but defining the mind defies a final definition because the mind is not fully understood. The mind is not exactly the brain though our brain is obviously the bodily organ that hosts the mind. That said, the best source of information concerning anything is to consult its creator. On matters that involve my iPhone, I consult Apple. On matters that involve ourselves and our minds, we should consult our Creator-- Almighty God, and His word, the Bible.

Biblically, the mind is also difficult to understand. The word "mind" is used in Old and New Testament languages of the Bible in many ways and within various contexts. For the purposes of this devotional, we will consider the definition of mind from Luke, 10:27, *So he answered and said, "You shall love the Lord your God with all your heart, with all your soul, with all your strength, and with all your **mind** and your neighbor as yourself."*

From this text, we will compile a definition of "mind" from two widely recognized resources for understanding biblical words; *Strong's Exhaustive Concordance of the Bible (Ref. G1271)* and *Vine's Expository Dictionary of New Testament Words (See Vine's notes)*. Here is a concise definition of mind from these two resources:

> *The faculty of moral reflection; the faculty of thinking; a way of thinking and feeling thoughts, either good or bad.*

From this definition, we can better appreciate how to love God with "all our mind." We love God through how we think, reflect, and by the feelings/actions our thoughts generate.

From this foundation, we will consider renewal and principles of change for a better life.

Reflection Question: What did you learn about the mind that you did not already know?

Key insight I gained today:

Today's action item based on insight:

Day 2
A Biblical Perspective on the Mind

1 Corinthians 2:13, *These things we also speak, not in words which man's wisdom teaches but which the Holy Spirit teaches, comparing spiritual things with spiritual. But the natural man does not receive the things of the Spirit of God, for they are foolishness to him; nor can he know them, because they are spiritually discerned.*

A major shift in thinking happened in the 20th Century that mirrors the rise of psychology and psychiatry. People today generally regard psychology and psychiatry as the authoritative source for all things mental. Ministers and Christian counselors are sometimes viewed as unhelpful by the scientific community (though some *are* unhelpful). After all is said and done scientifically, there remains a void in understanding humanity that only God and His word can fill, as it relates to the human heart and mind.

Nothing in our Christian faith is opposed to taking full advantage of expert science and medical help. In fact, we thank God for effective clinicians, doctors and medical professionals!

However, matters of the heart and the soul can only be rightly understood through the Scriptures. The mind is part of the soul. This devotional book unapologetically relies on God's Word to help believers in Christ, and all who seek Him, understand the mind from a biblical perspective.

Our thinking is shaped by two factors: 1) Man's wisdom, and 2) The Holy Spirit. The former is "natural" and the latter is "spiritual." As Christians, we don't consider man's wisdom necessarily wrong, but it is most certainly incomplete. Since the mind is clearly not something **natural**, man's **natural** wisdom is incapable of fully understanding the mind. All the more reason to rely on God and His word for understanding. Some things, like the mind, are "spiritually discerned."

Reflection Question: What is an example of man's wisdom that falls short of what the Holy Spirit can teach?

Key insight I gained today:

Today's action item based on insight:

Day 3
The Masterpiece Mindset

Ephesians 2:10, *For we are God's masterpiece. He has created us anew in Christ Jesus, so we can do the good things he planned for us long ago.*

When I was a young undergrad at John Herron Art School in Indianapolis, I did artistic painting. I used oil paints, linseed oil, and different kinds of brushes. Every painting started with a clean, empty canvas. I decided what subjects to paint, whether something from life such as objects or landscapes, or something from my imagination. The decision was mine to make.

Your mind is like a canvas. You are like a painter who can shape your reality and lifestyle through decisions and actions. God has provided all the "colors" and "brushes" (grace) needed to paint a beautiful portrait of a purposeful life.

A masterpiece does not happen by accident. It is not the result of something random. A masterpiece is the result of an inspired plan. We usually relate a masterpiece to artwork or some other work by an artist, writer, musician, architect, or craftsman. Essentially, a masterpiece is anyone's best work. Not "best" in relation to someone else's work, but only in relation to the master's work and potential.

Unfortunately, the canvas of life is sometimes marked up or painted over with another image that one did not choose. It's like having marked up paper as opposed to a clean sheet of paper. Sometimes people don't get to start with a clean canvas. What happened to us as children had great significance on our future. We all know this, which is why everyone wants a better future for his or her children.

What I call the "masterpiece mindset" is the recognition that you and I are the masterful work of God. **You are God's masterpiece....His best work!** You may not presently *feel* like a masterpiece, but feelings have never changed the reality of something or someone. Don't ask yourself how you *feel*. Ask yourself what you *believe*.

Renewing the mind is the best path towards adopting the masterpiece mindset and allowing the grace of God to reveal His master work to you and through you.

Reflection Question: As God's masterpiece creation, describe 1-3 of your qualities.

Key insight I gained today:

Today's action item based on insight:

Day 4
The Best Version of You

Ephesians 4:20, *But you have not so learned Christ, 21 if indeed you have heard Him and have been taught by Him, as the truth is in Jesus: 22 that you put off, concerning your former conduct, the old man which grows corrupt according to the deceitful lusts, 23 and be renewed in the spirit of your mind, 24 and that you put on the new man which was created according to God, in true righteousness and holiness.*

Reading the text above motivates me to ask the question: **"Am I the best version of myself?"** It is an odd question, but it is entirely appropriate in light of our greater potential. Life is lived on many levels, from social to professional, to physical, to marital, to financial, to spiritual, and more.

On every level, it is necessary to avoid complacency and separate our "lesser self" from unnecessary or ungodly behaviors that are limiting factors. Christ has already provided a firm foundation on which to build a fruitful life. The standard for a better life is recognizing the things we *"have been taught by Him [Jesus]."* In this letter to Christians, the Apostle Paul summarized the spiritual growth process as **"putting off"** and **"putting on."** It is interesting that Paul acknowledged the fact that Christians may still need to discard "former conduct."

The three keys to this process are:
1) Be renewed in the spirit (or attitude) of the mind.
2) Put off the "old man."
3) Put on the "new man," also called the "new you."

These are simple steps, but this is not something we can do in our own strength. As the text said, we should do what we have "learned from Christ." This is the value of our time in personal devotions, in Bible studies, and receiving the word of God from our pastors and teachers.

Reflection Question: What are 1-2 things that you need to "put off" and 1-2 things that you need to "put on?"

Key insight I gained today:

Today's action item based on insight:

Day 5
Renewed Mind: Where Transformation Happens

"And do not be conformed to this world, but be transformed by the renewing of your mind, that you may prove what is that good and acceptable and perfect will of God." Romans 12:2

Paul states that transformation takes place in a believer when something godly happens in his mind. One might think that complete transformation would have occurred when a person received Jesus as Lord. The new birth brings new life and a new spirit to our inner man. The word "transformation" literally means "a metamorphosis." We best understand metamorphosis in what occurs when a caterpillar becomes a butterfly. The caterpillar is the same insect as the butterfly, but it undergoes a complete transformation. This is a wonderful picture of Christian maturity. The caterpillar is not the person *before* Christ. This example represents the Christian's growth potential.

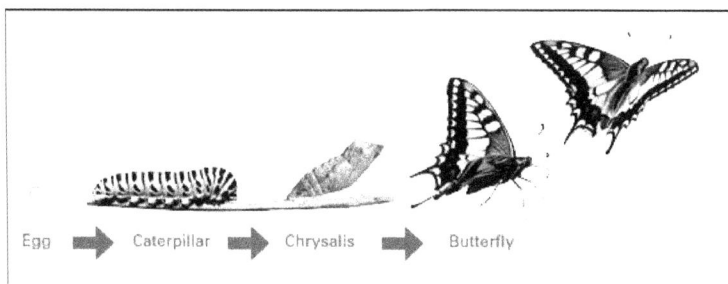

Egg ➡ Caterpillar ➡ Chrysalis ➡ Butterfly

Through renewing the mind, we go from one level of growth and maturity to another. In a matter of a few months or years each of us can experience a change so profound that we would appear to others like butterflies while knowing that we began as caterpillars.

You will show me the path of life; In Your presence is fullness of joy; At Your right hand are pleasures forevermore. (Psalm 16:11) One of the "paths of life" that we are learning here is the importance of renewing our mind.

Another way to think about renewal is in properly refinishing or restoring furniture. It's easy to spray paint over old wood. A proper restoration will involve removing the old finish and going down to the essence, bare wood. As new Christians, we begin as redeemed "furniture" needing refinishing and enhancement. Of course, a life is far more valuable and complex than furniture, but these examples aid our thinking about being renewed.

Reflection Question: As you continue to transform positively, what are you becoming?

Key insight I gained today:

Today's action item based on insight:

Day 6
Four-Step Process For Renewing the Mind

What God requires, He provides. Whatever God asks of you, He provides grace to fulfill that responsibility. Following are four suggested action items that summarize the process of renewing the mind. As James said, *"Faith without works* [corresponding action] *is dead being alone."* (James 2:17)

Step One

Read, listen to and receive messages inspired of the Word of God, the Bible. God's Word is the revelation of His plan and purpose for your life and humanity. The more acquainted with the Word you become, the more acclimated you become with God's way of doing things.

James 1:21 puts it this way, *"Therefore lay aside all filthiness and overflow of wickedness, and receive with meekness the implanted word, which is able to save your souls."*

The soul is comprised of our **mind**, will, and emotions. As the word is "implanted" into our minds, it displaces all contrary ideas and beliefs that are inconsistent with a Christ-centered life. The idea behind "implant" is to intentionally put something into a certain place, not unlike planting flowers around the house.

Step Two

Let the character of Christ be formed within through fellowship with Him, time in prayer, and growing through the trials and tests of life. Character requires constant development. What the old folks told you was true: "That which does not kill you makes you stronger!"

My little children, for whom I labor in birth again until Christ is formed in you (Gal. 4:19)

Like the apostle Paul, your pastor labors in teaching God's word to help "form" the character of Christ in you. This is similar to human development. You have the DNA but still must gain strength, knowledge, and skill to fulfill your potential.

Step Three

Worship, pray, and praise the Lord so that your mind will grow accustomed to this behavior. Though worship does not begin in the mind, our minds can be trained to cooperate and strongly participate in worship, prayer and praise. It is possible to arrive at a place where worship, prayer, and praise are not something you do only in church or when you're feeling "spiritual." It is something you simply want to do because it has become a part of you.

David learned this principle, *"O God, You are my God; Early will I seek You; My soul thirsts for You; My flesh longs for You In a dry and thirsty land Where there is no water."* (Psalm 63:1)

Step Four

Serve others and share the gospel of Jesus with hurting people. One of the best ways to remove selfishness from your life is to serve others. Serving others is usually inconvenient, but through serving we connect to God in a profound way.

Reflection Question: What have you heard or read over the past few days that has helped to renew your mind?

Key insight I gained today:

Today's action item based on insight:

Day 7
The Amazing Power of a Willing Mind

2 Corinthians 8:12, *For if there is first a willing mind, it is accepted according to what one has, and not according to what he does not have.*

Willingness is one of the most power principles of progress that you can activate. A willing mind opens your life to possibilities, provision, and power from God. A willing mind helps extend your ability beyond present limitations.

Looking at the first part of 2 Corinthians 8, the Apostle Paul provided an example of the power of willingness.

2 Corinthians 8:1 *Moreover, brethren, we make known to you the grace of God bestowed on the churches of Macedonia: 2 that in a great trial of affliction the abundance of their joy and their deep poverty abounded in the riches of their liberality. 3 For I bear witness that according to their ability, yes, and beyond their ability, they were freely willing,*

The believers in Macedonia showed the power of a willing mind. They were dealing with adverse circumstances and a *"great trial of affliction."* Because of willingness, Paul wrote that the Macedonia believers operated *"according to their ability"* as well as **"BEYOND their ability."** Cooperating with God-given assignments attracts His grace which results in increased ability. A willing mind is an **open** mind. As Jesus said, *"If you can believe, all things are possible."* (Mark 9:23)

We all face moments when we cannot see how to get something done or how to move forward. For a lack of willingness, we sometimes completely miss opportunities to change, advance, and experience a better life. The good news is that change, advancement, and a better life begins with the simple decision to be willing. A willing mind says, "Yes, by the Grace of God, I can do this!."

Reflection Question: What is one situation where having a willing mind will help??

Key insight I gained today:

Today's action item based on insight:

Day 8
New Things

We live in a world full of old things alongside new things. This does not present a problem until unnecessary old things blind us to new and better things. This is especially important in regards to liberating spiritual realities we can't embrace because of limiting past/present factors. God is infinite, ever-present, and is always nudging us toward a better tomorrow. God sent Jeremiah to share something that was very encouraging to Israel during a difficult time in their history:

For I know the thoughts that I think toward you, says the Lord, thoughts of peace and not of evil, to give you a future and a hope. (Jeremiah 29:11)

Notice the "new things" in this statement. Had they been people who were only looking at old things, they would have remained in their present state and missed the hopeful message that God sent. The good news is, God's message through Jeremiah is true for us today. What God thinks of you is always hopeful! Wrap your mind around the **hope** before you. Focus on what God is saying and doing and you will find solutions for your present challenges.

The following Scriptures express the **newness** that Jesus brings into your life. Read and reflect on the following Scriptures. Pay special attention to the words and phrases that indicate promises to be received or responsibilities to be followed.

Therefore we were buried with Him through baptism into death, that just as Christ was raised from the dead by the glory of the Father, even so we also should walk in newness of life. (Romans 6:4)

But now we have been delivered from the law, having died to what we were held by, so that we should serve in the newness of the Spirit and not in the *oldness of the letter. (*Romans 7:6)

He says: "Behold, the days are coming, says the Lord, when I will make a new covenant with the house of Israel and with the house of Judah... For this is the covenant that I will make with the house of Israel after those days, says the Lord: I will put My laws in their mind and write them on their hearts; and I will be their God, and they shall be My people..." (Hebrews 8:8, 10)

Therefore, brethren, having boldness to enter the Holiest by the blood of Jesus, by a new and living way which He consecrated for us, through the veil, that is, His flesh, and having a High Priest over the house of God, let us draw near with a true heart in full assurance of faith... (Hebrews 10:19-22)

Therefore, if anyone is in Christ, he is a new creation; old things have passed away; behold, all things have become new. (2 Corinthians 5:17)

Reflection Question: Describe the newness God has brought into your life.

Key insight I gained today:

Today's action item based on insight:

Day 9
A Steadfast Mind

Proverbs 16:3 , *Commit your works to the LORD, and your thoughts will be established.*

"Steadfast" is a beautiful word. It means, "firmly fixed in place; immovable; not subject to change; firm in belief, determination, or adherence."

A steadfast life is based on the firm foundation of Christ and a renewed mind. In a troubled and unstable world, being steadfast is a virtue that makes you stand out in a positive light. Cultivating a steadfast mind and life is one of the keys to success.

The following Scriptures provide inspiration and faith in God as it concerns becoming/being steadfast.

Therefore, my beloved brethren, be steadfast, immovable, always abounding in the work of the Lord, knowing that your labor is not in vain in the Lord. (I Corinthians 15:58)

You will keep him in perfect peace, Whose mind is stayed on You, Because he trusts in You. (Isaiah. 26:3)

Rejoicing in hope, patient in tribulation, continuing steadfastly in prayer, (Romans 12:12)

Create in me a clean heart, O God, And renew a steadfast spirit within me, (Psalm 51:10)

if indeed you continue in the faith, grounded and steadfast, and are not moved away from the hope of the gospel which you heard, which was preached to every creature under heaven, of which I, Paul, became a minister. (Colossians 1:23)

You therefore, beloved, since you know this beforehand, beware lest you also fall from your own steadfastness, being led away with the error of the wicked. (2 Peter 3:17)

Reflection Question: What are one or two steadfast factors in your life?

Key insight I gained today:

Today's action item based on insight:

Day 10
Fervent Prayer Begins in the Mind

James 5:16, *The effective, fervent prayer of a righteous man avails much.*

The earnest (heart-felt, continued) prayer of a righteous man makes tremendous power available-dynamic in its working. (James 5:16 Amplified Bible.)

The word "fervent" means "hot." Prayer is a spiritual action but it is in our mind that we decide when and how to pray. The power of prayer is not through our minds, but until the decision to pray is taken, nothing happens.

Prayer is the most fundamental action that a believer in Jesus Christ can perform. It is also the most important and effective means of communication with God available to mankind. Through prayer we tap into the very presence of God and into the realm of higher power and authority.

Prayer is to the Christian what contractors are to architects. Architects have the plan, but the contractor creates a building from lines, measurements and specifications on paper. We are commissioned to do the works of Jesus. We are following the plans of our Great Architect, God the Father. Through prayer we receive the revelation of what to do, where to do it, and how to do it. We also receive the necessary tools to carry out God's purposes in the earth. Furthermore, through prayer, we clear a path for God in our surroundings and within our hearts for God to do His work.

The simple truth is this: In a world of confusion and shifting standards, prayer is the one thing that is always the right thing to do. Prayer time is never wasted time. Prayer shapes our thinking and reasoning in essential ways.

Consider the key words from James 5:16,

1. **Effective** - having adequate power or force to produce the effect

2. **Fervent** - hot; glowing; intensely warm; vehement; animated; intense

3. **Righteous Man** - upright, virtuous, free from guilt or sin

Reflection Question: In addition to prayer, what is one thing that could become more effective if you became fervent about it?

Key insight I gained today:

Today's action item based on insight:

Day 11
The Awesome Power of a Good Mindset

Romans 8:5, *Those who live according to the flesh have their minds set on what the flesh desires; but those who live in accordance with the Spirit have their minds set on what the Spirit desires.*

What is a mindset? 1) It is a belief that affects someone's attitude. 2) A habitual or characteristic mental attitude that determines how you will interpret and respond to situations.

What is an attitude? 1) A personal view of something 2) A manner, disposition, feeling, position, etc., with regard to a person or thing; tendency or orientation of the mind.

Attitudes (a small thing) lead to mindsets (a big thing). If a person's attitude is consistently negative, this leads to an overall mindset of negativity that affects every part of his life. This is why we **should not** embrace a bad attitude, not even towards a single person or circumstance. A bad attitude is like mold: If it is not eliminated, it grows and adversely affects every space.

The only way to consistently live "in accordance with the Spirit" is to allow the Word and Spirit of God to change your thinking, habits, and behavior. Refusing this change and growth is both foolish and dangerous. More importantly, there is no good reason not to change for the better since grace has been given to us for that purpose.

Sometimes our patterns of thinking and habits may not please God, though seeming and feeling correct. Unchallenged concepts and ideas for which there is no scriptural foundation can lead to a faulty mindset. A faulty mindset can lead to self-deception, which is the act of believing something that is untrue.

Self-deception is something that is entirely "curable." We only need the light of truth. We are all learning, growing, and becoming wiser. Self-deception becomes dangerous when we close our minds to facts and objective truth. "Objective truth" refers to realities that have nothing to do with our feelings and opinions.

Reflection Question: What is one attitude you need to change to have a different mindset?

Key insight I gained today:

Today's action item based on insight:

Day 12
Next Level Thinking

1 Corinthians 2:12-16, *Now we have received, not the spirit of the world, but the Spirit who is from God, that we might know the things that have been freely given to us by God. These things we also speak, not in words which man's wisdom teaches but which the Holy Spirit teaches, comparing spiritual things with spiritual. 14 But the natural man does not receive the things of the Spirit of God, for they are foolishness to him; nor can he know them, because they are spiritually discerned. But he who is spiritual judges all things, yet he himself is rightly judged by no one. For "Who has known the mind of the Lord that he may instruct Him?" But we have the mind of Christ.*

We often hear the phrase, "Go to the next level." We recognize the term as a challenge to go higher and be better. There are few things better than going to a higher level of thinking.

In life, we are trained to think according to educational systems, family values, cultural norms, and according to various signals received from marketing, expectations of others, and much more. Religious training (as distinct from a growing relationship with Christ) too often involves shaping one's thinking according to traditional and non-biblical practices. Much of our educational and religious training amounts to practices and thinking which Paul attributes to "the natural man." This level of thinking is not capable of understanding the things of God.

At the next level, we become rooted in godly and biblical realities on which to build our concepts and ideals. The strength of next level thinking comes from a relationship with the person of Jesus and the indwelling Spirit of God.

Prov. 14:12, *There is a way that seems right to a man, but in the end it leads to death.*

Thinking and reasoning on a faulty basis can have bad consequences which are not always outwardly evident. When we learn how to think on the next level, with Christ at the center, we develop a better basis for understanding life and ourselves. Life makes more sense and hope rises.

Reflection Question: Is there anything in your culture that conflicts with the wisdom of God?

Key insight I gained today:

Today's action item based on insight:

Day 13
Victory Over Problems With The Mind

2 Corinthians 2:14, N*ow thanks be to God who always leads us in triumph in Christ, and through us diffuses the fragrance of His knowledge in every place.*

There are many types of problems that are rooted in our behaviors and thinking. It is important not to underestimate the grace and wisdom of God when facing difficulties. This is not to exclude getting help from others, but to encourage us to never leave God outside of the problems we face.

Being transformed by the renewing of the mind brings victory over many types of problems that stem from the mind. **Expect** freedom and mastery over the following problems:

Heaviness: A depressed feeling caused by thinking on bad situations, having regrets, reviewing mistakes or dwelling on relationships that have gone sour.

Evil thoughts: Sinful thoughts of all types including sexual fantasies, malice or dishonest schemes

Vain imaginations: Completely useless thinking such as wondering what it would be like to live one's life as another person.

Envy/Jealousy: Being grieved at the success of others or becoming too possessive of others.

Comparisons: Making value judgments about yourself based upon what others have or have not done.

Fear: Living in expectation of danger and harm

Distractions: Getting easily side-tracked from important tasks by unimportant issues and events.

Presumption: Prematurely forming opinions or judgments about people and situations

Pride of opinion: Unwilling to listen or accept correction and direction from others

For each of these problems, there is grace from God to help us overcome.

Reflection Question: What are 1-3 problems that you need to (and will) overcome from the list above?

Key insight I gained today:

Today's action item based on insight:

Day 14
A Decision that Stills the Storm

Sometimes inner questions and conflicts rage like a storm. The Apostle Paul described his experience, which will seem very familiar to many of us. Note Paul's honesty in sharing about his "storm."

For what I am doing, I do not understand. For what I will to do, that I do not practice; but what I hate, that I do. If, then, I do what I will not to do, I agree with the law that it is good. But now, it is no longer I who do it, but sin that dwells in me. For I know that in me (that is, in my flesh) nothing good dwells; for to will is present with me, but how to perform what is good I do not find. For the good that I will to do, I do not do; but the evil I will not to do, that I practice. Now if I do what I will not to do, it is no longer I who do it, but sin that dwells in me. I find then a law, that evil is present with me, the one who wills to do good. (Romans 7:15-21)

Here is how Paul resolved his issue:

For I delight in the law of God according to the inward man .... I thank God through Jesus Christ our Lord! So then, with the mind I myself serve the law of God, but with the flesh the law of sin. (Romans 7:22, 25)

Paul did not "cave in" to his feelings and urges, but nor did he deny them. He recognized two realities: 1) The "flesh" (which is our human nature absent God) is always committed to going the wrong way. 2) Making a decision with one's mind to serve the "law of God" (The Word of God) changes one's focus and position to a place of victory!

It is not "mind over matter." It is "mind on God" that makes the difference.

Reflection Question: What decision can you make that will stop an inner conflict in your life?

Key insight I gained today:

Today's action item based on insight:

Day 15
In God's Image & Likeness

1 Thessalonians 5:23, *Now may the God of peace Himself sanctify you completely; and may your whole spirit, soul, and body be preserved blameless at the coming of our Lord Jesus Christ.*

Genesis 1:27, *We were created in God's image and likeness. So God created man in His own image; in the image of God He created him; male and female He created them.*

God is Father, Son, and Holy Spirit. Because people are created in His image and likeness, we reflect His Triune image in possessing a spirit, a soul, and a body. In reality, we **are** a spirit, we **have** a soul and we **live in** a body.

You are God's Masterpiece!

Jesus said, *"That which is born of the flesh is flesh and that which is born of the Spirit is spirit."* (John 3:6)

The Christian life begins with a "new birth" within the human spirit. Believers in Christ should live from the "inside-out." Religious and "carnal" living is focused on living from the "outside-in."

Your soul is the most distinctive part of "you." Your body expresses the life of your spirit and soul to the world around you and displays the focus of your life, whether for God or not.

The "mind" is the master of the soul. The mind must be "renewed" and oriented towards godly living.

And do not be conformed to this world, but be transformed by the renewing of your mind... (Romans 12:2)

©Bryan Hudson, Th.B., M.S.

Because God is a spirit, and we are made in His image, this makes us spiritual beings. This explains the fascination that people have with "extra-sensory," or "para-normal" experi-

35

ences. The key to avoiding confusion or deception in spiritual things is to get an understanding about these realities from God's Word, not from the fragments of people's opinions and feelings.

Life is too important to misunderstand or be misled with lesser information.

Reflection Question: Why is your spirit the strongest part of you?

Key insight I gained today:

Today's action item based on insight:

Day 16
How to Love With Your Mind

Matthew 22:37, *Jesus said to him, "You shall love the Lord your God with all your heart, with all your soul, and with all your **mind**."*

We usually think of love as something emotional or romantic. This perspective is accurate as it relates to our emotions and desires. However, the love that Jesus spoke about is the highest form of love. We can call it, "The God kind of love." This is the love that motivated God to send Jesus to offer Himself to redeem us from our sins.

This God kind of love is very profound and provides an unselfish motivation. Jesus described love as something that extends past emotions and self-serving motivations.

The love of God engages all parts of our personhood, spirit, soul, and body. This kind of love is less like riding a bicycle that uses *some* muscles. It is more like swimming which is a physical activity that engages almost *all* of one's muscles.

How do we love with our minds? Let's return to our original definition of the mind:

> *The faculty of moral reflection; the faculty of thinking; a way of thinking and feeling thoughts, either good or bad.*

We love God through how we think, reflect, and by the feelings/actions our thoughts generate.

Our thoughts and decisions lead towards actions that demonstrate love, which is more than intentions and feelings.

Reflection Question: What are 1-2 examples of walking in the God kind of love?

Key insight I gained today:

Today's action item based on insight:

Day 17
Tighten Up Your Thinking

1 Peter 1:13, *Therefore gird up the loins of your mind, be sober, and rest your hope fully upon the grace that is to be brought to you at the revelation of Jesus Christ.*

Your loins are the pelvic region of your body. In ancient times "girding the loins" meant to gather up long garments and tighten them around your hips and waist so that you could run, fight or do something productive.

Have you ever seen a young man trying to run with his pants sagging? Have you ever had the experience of getting a loose garment caught on something? This is the idea of girding your loins.

Therefore, to *"gird up the loins of your mind"* is to put your mind and thinking in a position to be useful to the Spirit of God, and not merely for selfish aims. The text also stated, "Be sober" and to rest fully on the grace of God. Sober means "serious and focused."

Most of us have had the experience in school of having to become serious and focus our thinking in order to do well with a class and especially to take a test.

We can use the same approach in regards to how we think and get things done in life.

Reflection Question: What do you need to focus on right now?

Key insight I gained today:

Today's action item based on insight:

Day 18
The Necessity of Simplicity

2 Corinthians. 11:3; B*ut I fear, lest somehow, as the serpent deceived Eve by his craftiness, so your minds may be corrupted from the simplicity that is in Christ.*

When I was in graduate school, I once complained to a professor about the unfairness of an exam I had taken. I explained to him my concern about a couple of questions on the exam being unclear and permitting multiple answers. I will never forget what he said to me. He said, "Bryan, you were *overthinking* the questions."

On further reflection, I had to admit that he was right. Rather than see the question in its simplicity, I added complexity to the questions and frustrated myself. This is exactly what happened in the garden of the Eden. God gave Adam and Eve very clear instructions. The serpent came along and distracted Eve, and Adam also who was standing idly by watching the whole thing happen.

Distractions to God's purposes and instruction for our lives still come the same way. Whether coming from Satan or through life's circumstances, we can find ourselves thinking incorrectly, like missing an instruction at the airport and winding up at the wrong gate waiting for the wrong flight.

The old saying is true, "Keep it simple."

Reflection Question: What has become complicated in your life that you need to simplify?

Key insight I gained today:

Today's action item based on insight:

Day 19
Having Unity of Purpose

1 Peter 3:8; *Finally, all of you be of one mind, having compassion for one another; love as brothers, be tenderhearted, be courteous.*

In covenant relationships it is very important to be of one mind with the person or persons with whom you live and work. By "covenant relationships," I'm referring to interpersonal contexts like marriage, church membership, team projects, and such. Being of "one mind" does not suggest uniformity, it suggests unity of purpose.

Unity of purpose is a very powerful principle. It is the common denominator among all successful groups of people. We use our minds, not to distract from the larger purpose, but to add our distinctiveness to that purpose and enhance successful outcomes. Sometimes people think they're doing their group a service by playing "the devil's advocate" or by raising contrarian points of view. This approach is actually counterproductive and requires less intelligence than thinking creatively about ways to contribute to the success of the common purpose.

Being "one mind" is not compromising to the point of setting aside what you think. It is using your mind to find a solution that supports a greater common purpose. There will also be time to pursue personal interests. But the greatest satisfaction and peace of mind comes when working towards collective purposes and balancing personal preferences with the greater good.

Reflection Question: What can you do to help a collective purpose with which you are involved?

Key insight I gained today:

Today's action item based on insight:

Day 20
Harness Your Imagination

2 Corinthians 10:5, *Casting down arguments and every high thing that exalts itself against the knowledge of God, bringing every thought into captivity to the obedience of Christ.*

Our imagination is often both the best and worst power that we possess. Imagination is one of the distinctive qualities of the human mind. The ability to see things and envision programs and processes is one of the marks that we are created by God. This is one of the abilities that God has on an infinitely powerful level. We share in that divine ability to imagine and take action.

We are all very aware of the tragic outcomes of human imagination. One example would be the third Reich under Adolf Hitler. This insidious imagination of one man resulted in the extermination of millions of Jewish people, the loss of tens of thousands of American and allied lives in fighting a war to stop this man's imagination.

On the positive side, we know about the imagination of Rev. Dr. Martin Luther King, Jr., who envisioned a better American society in his famous speech, *"I have a dream."* His positive imagination, in cooperation with thousands of other people, black and white, transformed our nation in profound ways.

Your imagination benefits from a renewed mind. A mind that is surrendered to Christ and trained according to God's word will lead to a life that does great and beneficial things.

Reflection Question: What are your two greatest dreams to accomplish in life?

Key insight I gained today:

Today's action item based on insight:

Day 21
Win the Battle: Flesh vs. Spirit

Galatians 5:16-17, *"I say then: Walk in the Spirit, and you shall not fulfill the lust of the flesh. For the flesh lusts against the Spirit, and the Spirit against the flesh; and these are contrary to one another, so that you do not do the things that you wish."*

In biblical terms the soul lies between the spirit and the body (human nature or "flesh"). As a result your soul (mind, will and emotions) is "pulled" in two directions--either by the Spirit of God or by our human nature (flesh). For example, we can think both sinful thoughts or holy thoughts (our mind). We can desire to do something self-destructive or we can desire to do something that saves lives (our will). We can feel like quitting or we can feel like praising God (our emotions).

Having conflicting thoughts, desires and emotions is not something that we "get over" because it is part of our human nature until Christ returns. Renewing our minds will reduce the severity of these conflicting thoughts as we learn to *"walk in the Spirit."* We must be intentional when it comes to renewing the mind and staying in the presence of God.

Developing and maintaining a healthy mind is not an involuntary action like breathing. It is a voluntary act like eating healthy foods.

Winner's Affirmations:

By the grace of God, I am what I am

I honor people at all levels of life
Winning with God is my priority
I give God the glory and I put in the work
Helping others helps me
I will not gain the world and lose my soul
I can do more than I've done before
I might be young, but don't underestimate me
I might be an old dog, but I still learn lots of tricks
I have the "rage to master"
I am not a quitter and I don't "half step"

Reflection Question: What is one way to think that help you walk more in the Spirit?

Key insight I gained today:

Today's action item based on insight:

Day 22
Setting the Mind: A Winning Strategy

Colossians 3:1-3, *If then you were raised with Christ, seek those things which are above, where Christ is, sitting at the right hand of God.* **Set your mind** *on things above, not on things on the earth. For you died, and your life is hidden with Christ in God.*

Romans 8:5, *For those who live according to the flesh set their minds on the things of the flesh, but those who live according to the Spirit,* **[set their minds on]** *the things of the Spirit.*

You have the ability to choose your thoughts and make decisions. You can command yourself to take action empowered by the Holy Spirit and grace of God. Following are suggestions of affirmations you can say aloud in conjunction with prayer. This is consistent with Scriptures such as 2 Corinthians 4:13, *And since we have the same spirit of faith, according to what is written, "I believed and therefore I spoke," we also believe and therefore speak...*

1. Mortify my mind • Romans 8:5-8, 12-14
"Carnality does not control my lifestyle. My mind is the property of Jesus. Satan, keep your hands off! I am dead to sin and alive to God. I am dead to things carnal and alive to things spiritual. I am a debtor to the Holy Spirit who gave me life."

2. Clear my mind • 1 John 3:11-12
"I clear from my mind of thoughts of anger, envy and disappointment at others. I give place for the peace of God to flood my mind. Jesus, you are my peace. I dig up seeds of bitterness and cast them away. I have the mind of Christ." (Hebrews 12:14-15; 1 Corinthians 2:16)

3. Renew my mind • Ephesians 4:23
"I have the power through my Lord Jesus Christ to replace wrong thought patterns with thoughts that please God. I can root out, pluck down, throw down and destroy anything in me that is not of God. I can build and plant anything that is of God." (Jeremiah. 1:10)

4. Set my mind • Colossians 3:1-4
"I am a decisive person by the grace of God. My mind taps into the riches of God's wisdom, knowledge and understanding. My mind is innovative, creative and productive in every purpose of God. I and disciplined in my thought life and repel every fiery dart from Satan."

5. Focus my mind • Romans 6:16-18
"I see clearly what I must do. There is no cloud of confusion in me. My mind will grasp everything I need to know. I cast down imaginations and opinions born of pride. My mind is the tool and servant of my Lord Jesus Christ!"

6. Guard my mind • Proverbs 4:10-26
"I guard my mind from the seeds of Satan. My mind is the gateway to my heart and I will protect the treasure of God's Word in me. The cares of this world; the deceitfulness of riches; and the lusts of other things will not choke the Word in me. God's healing power dominates my body and mind. The forces of the life of God flow out of me to bless others." (Mark 4:19)

Reflection Question: Which 1-2 affirmations above were the most significant to you today?

Key insight I gained today:

Today's action item based on insight:

Day 23
The Life-Changing Power of Solitude

1 Samuel 62:5, *My soul, wait silently for God alone, For my expectation is from Him.*

Isaiah 30:15, *For thus says the Lord God, the Holy One of Israel: "In returning and rest you shall be saved; in quietness and confidence shall be your strength." But you would not, 16] and you said, "No, for we will flee on horses"--therefore you shall flee! And, "We will ride on swift horses"--therefore those who pursue you shall be swift!*

Confusion, nervousness, instability, and distraction are common problems among people today – including Christians. We have become a non-stop, noisy, and distracted society. We pay a high price for neglecting solitude in the presence of God.

1. Our lives become ordered by the pace and practice of this world and not by God.
2. We experience bewilderment, disorientation, and random thoughts – like a machine that is operated outside of its tolerances.
3. We become prone to misunderstanding people and purposes because of a lack of personal, inward focus.
4. We feed on noise and clamor – becoming addicted to confusion and preferring it over quiet.

Jesus gave us the perfect example of human existence according to divine order. His entire ministry was birthed and sustained out of the crucible of solitude and silence – He could know His Father's direction no other way. His preparedness to minister and the level of anointing upon Him was in direct proportion to His solitary time with the Father and with His own thoughts. Jesus lived a life of devotion to God interspersed with periods of ministering to others – not the reverse. Jesus began His ministry in the wilderness, in solitude, gaining strength for what lie ahead. When Satan came to tempt Him, he was at His strongest point, not His weakest point.

"Very early in the morning, while it was still dark, Jesus got up, left the house and went off to a solitary place, where he prayed." (Mark 1:35)

"Because so many people were coming and going that they did not even have a chance to eat, [Jesus] said to [his disciples], 'Come with me by yourselves to a quiet place and get some rest.' So they went away by themselves in a boat to a solitary place." (Mark 6:31-32)

"Jesus constantly sought solitude from the time of his baptism up to the Garden of Gethsemane, when He even went apart from those he took there to watch with him. It is solitude alone that opens the possibility of a radical relationship to God that can withstand all external events up to and beyond death." (Dallas Willard, *The Spirit of the Disciplines*)

Jesus was not driven by the needs of people, but by the purpose of God. Because of this Jesus gained the power to meet the needs of people in a dramatic, miraculous fashion. If He labored with people more than spent time with God, he would not have been as successful, and neither are we. Because Jesus spent time with God, His times of public ministry were dramatic and miraculous. He got more done in a shorter period of time.

Matthew 12:19, *He will not quarrel nor cry out, nor will anyone hear His voice in the streets. (*"...neither shall any man hear his voice above the street noise"* NAS)

Reflection Question: What is your plan for solitude with God?

Key insight I gained today:

Today's action item based on insight:

Day 24

Ears to Hear, Part One,
"Take Heed What & How You Hear"

Mark 4:23-25, *"If anyone has ears to hear, let him hear." And He said to them, "Take heed what you hear. With the same measure you use, it will be measured to you; and to you who hear, more will be given. For whoever has, to him more will be given; but whoever does not have, even what he has will be taken away from him."*

I once preached a message in which I used 1 Peter 4:12 as my text which reads, *"Beloved, do not think it strange concerning the fiery trial which is to try you, as though some strange thing happened to you."* In the message, I stressed the importance of understanding that trials and tests are a normal part of life, according to 1 Peter 4:12, thus we should not consider challenges a "strange" thing.

The message seemed to be well received with many people nodding their heads in approval saying, "Amen, Amen!" I felt assured that my audience understood the message. Soon after the service concluded, one of my parishioners asked to speak with me. She shared, "Pastor, pray for me. What I have been dealing with is so strange...it doesn't make sense." I asked her if she had understood the part of the message that addressed not considering "fiery trials" to be something "strange." She said that she *listened* to the entire message. I thought to myself, "You were listening to the message, but did not *hear* the Word." I encouraged her to listen to a recording of the message and review the Scriptures to have "ears to hear."

Listening and hearing are not always the same thing. The fact is many people do not hear—not just in church, but in many areas of life. Listening is a natural, physical ability. Hearing must be cultivated through training one's heart and mind to focus on what is being said and take it seriously.

Romans 10:17 says, *Faith itself comes by hearing; "Faith comes by hearing and hearing by the Word of God."* Listening is the act that leads to hearing when we focus our hearts on the Lord. When you **hear** Father God it brings a special type of confidence that we call faith.

Reflection Question: What do you need to start "hearing" that you've only been listening to?

Key insight I gained today:

Today's action item based on insight:

Day 25
Ears to Hear, Part Two,
"The Benefits of Hearing"

- How you hear will determine the quality of your life.

- How you hear will determine your level of authority and responsibility in life.

- How you hear will determine the measure of God's anointing on your life.

- Hearing determines aptitude (ability). *"If anyone has ears to hear, let him hear."*

Jesus said we must have "ears to hear." This indicates our willingness to hear instruction and direction. Many people fall short before they ever get started because they are not willing to hear, not willing to make a commitment to excellence, and not willing to move out of familiar territory.

Jesus never forced people to listen to Him or follow Him. He invited people to participate with Him and receive the blessing of God. Many times, Jesus began a teaching with the statement *"He who has ears to hear, let him hear."* This was His invitation to people who were serious. He proceeded to teach and afterwards waited for a response. Many of the people walked away, others were bewildered, but some lingered and inquired further of the things Jesus taught. These were the people who received the most from what he said. It was true then and is true now.

Jesus invites everyone to hear and know Him, but He lets our decision to hear determine the degree of understanding and fruitfulness we experience.

"And if anyone hears My words and does not believe, I do not judge him; for I did not come to judge the world but to save the world. He who rejects Me, and does not receive My words, has that which judges him--the word that I have spoken will judge him in the last day. (John 12:47-48)

A lack of hearing, or hearing the wrong things, will hamper your ability to walk in the full blessing and opportunities of life. For example, those who want to become medical doctors must spend countless hours hearing and reflecting upon what they have heard in the context of medicine. Simply being in the classroom passively listening won't do. You certainly don't want a doctor who was not paying attention while in school! In reality, any profession, task, or endeavor requires a full commitment to having "ears to hear." These are the people who excel in life and in fellowship with God.

Reflection Question: What have you missed for lack of hearing?

Key insight I gained today:

Today's action item based on insight:

Day 26

Ears to Hear, Part Three,
"Types of Listening That Lead to Hearing"

Hebrews 2:1, *Therefore we must give the more earnest heed to the things we have heard, lest we drift away.*

What measure of hearing do you use? That is, to what degree do you open your mind and heart to hear instruction and direction? There are four ways in which all of us choose to listen, which affects how we hear.

Passive Listening • Passive means, "not active, but acted upon." Passive people are generally sluggish and disengaged—believing that "whatever will be, will be." Passive listeners only "perk up" when something is said that has the promise of easing their burdens or bringing more comfort into their lives.

A passive listener is the kind of person who ignores the importance of changing the oil in his automobile every 3000-5000 miles. Passive listeners tend to take action when trouble arises. Passive listeners tend not to act until they are acted upon. Passive listeners labor under a great number of self-inflicted problems.

Convenient Listening • Convenient is defined as, "Situated within easy reach." The convenient listener only applies his heart to hear when the information or task is within easy reach. The best things in life are not usually within easy reach. We should not live with a sense of entitlement. We should live with a sense of purpose and responsibility.

Jesus says something that sounds strange on first hearing, "*And from the days of John the Baptist until now the kingdom of heaven suffers violence, and the violent take it by force*" (John 11:12). He was not talking about physical violence in this text. He was talking about being willing to take action. We call it being "proactive." Convenient listeners do not embrace this approach to life.

Reflection Question: What areas of passive or convenient listening need to be corrected?

Key insight I gained today:

Today's action item based on insight:

Day 27
Ears to Hear, Part Four,
"Types of Listening that Lead to Hearing"

Critical Listening • The word "critical" is defined as, "exhibiting the spirit of one who looks for and points out faults and defects." Communication often fails because of critical listening that is more concerned about finding faults than in understanding the content and meaning of the message. Critical listeners are not motivated to learn and grow. Critical listeners often develop a self-righteous attitude that seeks to obtain or maintain a superior position. At the same time, such persons are often frustrated with others for not listening to them. Jesus addressed this condition:

"For with what judgment you judge, you will be judged; and with the same measure you use, it will be measured back to you and why do you look at the speck in your brother's eye, but do not consider the plank in your own eye?" (Matthew 7:2-3)

Active Listening • Active listening allows us to hear without the limitations of passive, convenient, or critical listening. This should be our goal. "Active" is defined as: "Not waiting to be acted upon. Prepared to apply what is heard and act on it—regardless of the circumstances."

James 1:25 says, *"But he who looks into the perfect law of liberty and continues in it, and is not a forgetful hearer but a doer of the work, this one will be blessed in what he does."*

Active listeners always hear because **they are prepared to do** what they have heard. According to James, such persons are "blessed" in their efforts. People who rise to positions of authority and responsibility are usually those who have learned to be active listeners. People of strong faith have learned how to listen to God, meditate on the Word of God and allow the Holy Spirit to lead them in every endeavor of life. Again, *"So then faith comes by hearing, and hearing by the Word of God."* (Romans 10:17)

Reflection Question: What are 1-2 ways that you are going to practice active listening?

Key insight I gained today:

Today's action item based on insight:

Day 28
Established Thoughts, Established Life

Philippians 4:8, *Finally, brethren, whatever things are true, whatever things are noble, whatever things are just, whatever things are pure, whatever things are lovely, whatever things are of good report, if there is any virtue and if there is anything praiseworthy—meditate on these things.*

Commit your works to the LORD, and your thoughts will be established. (Proverbs 16:3)

Thinking works like a thermostat. You set the temperature and the device signals the HVAC to turn on and distribute either heating or cooling. More than any other factor, how we think regulates our environment and either stabilizes or destabilizes our lives.

Factors that affect us have two sources: Extrinsic and Intrinsic. Extrinsic means, "Coming from the outside of something." Intrinsic means, "Belonging to the essential nature of a thing: occurring as a natural part of something."

Circumstances like your work environment, economic state, or actions of other people are all extrinsic factors that you cannot always control. Thinking is an intrinsic factor that you can entirely control. I once heard a person say, "When you change, your circumstances will change." I did not agree with the statement until I considered the power of thinking and living in the presence of God.

"Commitment" happens first in the heart. According to Proverbs, commitment leads to established thoughts. Combining instructions form Philippians and Proverbs, it is easy to see the benefits of thinking positively.

Reflection Question: What extrinsic factors can you control or change to support better thinking?

Key insight I gained today:

Today's action item based on insight:

Day 29
The Mind of Christ: Thinking on a Higher Level

Jesus asked His disciples a question they could not answer from their intellect alone.

Matthew 16:13 When Jesus came into the region of Caesarea Philippi, He asked His disciples, saying, **"Who do men say that I, the Son of Man, am?"** *14 So they said, "Some say John the Baptist, some Elijah, and others Jeremiah or one of the prophets." 15 He said to them,* **"But who do you say that I am?"** *16 Simon Peter answered and said, "You are the Christ, the Son of the living God." 17 Jesus answered and said to him, "Blessed are you, Simon Bar-Jonah, for flesh and blood has not revealed this to you, but My Father who is in heaven.*

Most of the disciples could only compare Jesus with people they could think about, like John the Baptist or Elijah. However, Peter **reached beyond his intellect** to receive information from God. This was an example of having the Mind of Christ.

The only person who can tell us about God is the Spirit of God.

1 Corinthians 2:14 But the natural man does not receive the things of the Spirit of God, for they are foolishness to him; nor can he know them, because they are spiritually discerned. 15 But he who is spiritual judges all things, yet he himself is rightly judged by no one. 16 For "Who has known the mind of the Lord that he may instruct Him?" **But we have the mind of Christ.**

If we live only by what is familiar, we will be unable to handle the greater challenges and opportunities of life. Operating in the Mind of Christ is the single most important factor to understand the ways of God and living in consistent victory.

What is the mind of Christ?

The mind of Christ represents special grace to share in the thoughts, plans and motives of God.

Having the Mind of Christ is one of the benefits of being a Christian. *He who is joined to the Lord is one spirit with Him.* (1 Corinthians 6:17)

This is the reason that the task of renewing the mind is so essential. We cannot have the mind of Christ apart from renewing our mind. When we learn to think on a higher level, we will be able to live on a higher level.

Reflection Question: What are two examples of the mind of Christ active in your life?

Key insight I gained today:

Today's action item based on insight:

Day 30
Reflections on Change for a Better Life

Joshua 1:8, *This Book of the Law [the Word of God] shall not depart from your mouth, but you shall meditate on it day and night, so that you may be careful to do according to all that is written in it. For then you will make your way prosperous, and then you will have good success.*

Congratulations! You've reached the conclusion of this devotional book, but not the end of your journey. Use this final day to review the principles you have learned and the decisions you've taken.

Wrapping Up
1. Look over your daily notes and comments.
2. Pray, asking God for wisdom and a plan to follow through on what your have gained.
3. Think about people you can help grow stronger or find new life in Christ.
4. Praise God and celebrate His goodness in your life!
5. Use the link below or send me an email with your testimony about how this book and devotional process has blessed you.

Online Form: My Testimony of Change and a Better Life
www.BryanHudson.com
Email: *Testimony@VisionBooksMedia.com*

About the Author

Rev. Bryan Hudson has a multifaceted ministry and professional expertise focused on inspiring and empowering people to know God and achieve the best in their lives. Bryan's training has enabled him to merge ministry with media: Th.B. (Theology), B.S. (Media Arts & Science), M.S. (Education: Instructional Systems Technology).

As a writer, educator, producer, and Bible teacher, Bryan communicates insights on important issues and technologies to deliver solutions to people in need as well as equip leaders to effectively serve their organizations and communities.

He is the founder and senior pastor of *New Covenant Church & Ministries* in Indianapolis, Indiana. Bryan also directs *Vision Communications*, a progressive multimedia firm that creates cutting-edge traditional media and new media. He has conducted 15 summer multimedia training workshops for young men and women to equip and inspire them to use new media in positive ways. Bryan has ministered on the African continent on four occasions and helped establish a Christian training program in Lagos, Nigeria.

As an instructional designer and former adjunct professor, Bryan Hudson developed and taught a 300-level course at *Crossroads Bible College* in Indianapolis, *New Media for Urban Ministry*.
Bryan is married to Patricia Hudson, a public school educator. They have four grown children and reside in Indianapolis, Indiana.

Twitter: @ChurchMediaGuy
BryanHudson.com
VisionBooksMedia.com
NewCovenant.org
VisioncomSolutions.com

Other Books by Bryan Hudson

Available on Amazon.com & VisionBooksMedia.com

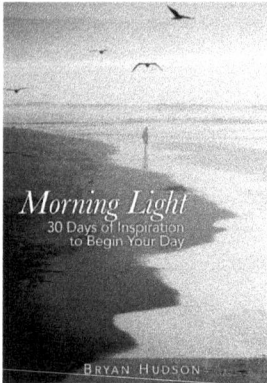

Morning Light
30 Days of Inspiration
to Begin Your Day

BRYAN HUDSON

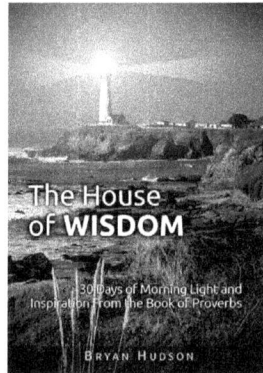

The House
of **WISDOM**

30 Days of Morning Light and
Inspiration from the Book of Proverbs

BRYAN HUDSON

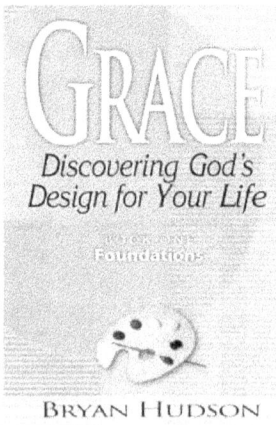

GRACE
*Discovering God's
Design for Your Life*

Foundations

BRYAN HUDSON

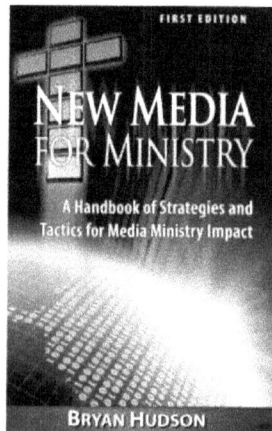

FIRST EDITION

NEW MEDIA
FOR MINISTRY

A Handbook of Strategies and
Tactics for Media Ministry Impact

BRYAN HUDSON

www.ingramcontent.com/pod-product-compliance
Lightning Source LLC
Chambersburg PA
CBHW071849020426
42331CB00007B/1921